WORKING AND EARNING FROM HOME

GET STARTED AND LIVE YOUR DREAMS

by

JOHN CONTON

Copyright@ the year 2020

All right reserved.

This write-up is subject to copyright policy. All rights are reserved, whether the entire or component of the material, particularly the rights of transformation, reprinting, recycle of illustration, reading, broadcasting, duplicate on microfilm or in any other way.
All right reserved. No part or even the whole of this book or contents may be produced or even transmitted or reproduced in any way, be it electronic or paper form or by any means, electronic or mechanical, also include recording or by any information storage or retrieval system, without prior written permission of the copyright owner..

Table of Contents

INTRODUCTION   8

CHAPTER 1   9

STARTING A BUSINESS   9

HOW PREPARED ARE YOU TO START A BUSINESS?   9
AM NOT AN INDUSTRIALIST?   9
WHY FEAR OF STARTING A BUSINESS?   10

SOME OF THE PURPOSE WHY YOU SHOULD START A BUSINESS.   11

CHAPTER 2   15

BUSINESS IDEAS   15

HOW TO FIND BUSINESS IDEAS.   15

SITUATION AND GOAL.   15
INTERESTS AND PASSIONS.   16
TRENDS AND NEEDS.   16
CREATING YOUR BUSINESS IDEAS.   17
NARROWING YOUR OPTIONS.   17
TESTING YOUR BUSINESS IDEAS.   17

SOURCES OF BUSINESS IDEAS   18

EXAMINE YOUR OWN SKILL SET FOR BUSINESS IDEAS: 18

KEEP UP WITH CURRENT EVENT:	**18**
INVENT NEW PRODUCT OR SERVICE:	**19**
ADD VALUE TO AN EXISTING PRODUCT:	**20**
INVESTIGATE OTHER MARKETS:	**20**
IMPROVE EXISTING PRODUCT OR SERVICES:	**20**
GET ON THE BANDWAGON:	**21**
TIPS FOR COMING UP WITH BUSINESS IDEAS	**21**
HOW TO COME UP WITH A GREAT BUSINESS IDEAS.	**22**
START WITH WHAT YOU LOVE:	**22**
START WITH SOMETHING PEOPLE NEED:	**22**
START WITH A TWIST:	**23**
START WITH SOMETHING YOU CAN TEST:	**23**
START WITH SOMETHING YOU CAN DO WITH SIDE.	**24**
CHAPTER 3	**26**
BUSINESS ENTITY AND TYPES	**26**
CLASSES OF BUSINESS	**26**
1. Service Business	26
2. Merchandising Business	27
CLASSES OF BUSINESS ORGANIZATION	**28**
1. Sole Proprietorship	28
COOPERATIVE	**30**

FURTHERMORE:	**31**
ASSOCIATION	31
ESTATE	31
JOINT iVENTURE	31
LIMITED iLIABILITY iLIMITED iPARTNERSHIP i(LLLP)	31
LIMITED iLIABILITY iPARTNERSHIP i(LLP)	32
LIMITED iPARTNERSHIP	32
MASSACHUSETTS iTRUST	32
MUNICIPALITY	33
NON-PROFIT iCORPORATION	33
PROFESSIONAL iLIMITED iLIABILITY iPARTNERSHIP i(PLLP)	33
TENANTS iIN iCOMMON	33
TRUST	33

CHAPTER i4 — 35

BUSINESS iPLANNING — 35

WHAT iIS iA iBUSINESS iPLAN?	35
REASON iFOR iA iBUSINESS iPLAN.	35
WHY iPREPARE iA iBUSINESS iPLAN	37
CONTENT iOF iA iBUSINESS iPLAN	37
ANALYSIS iOF iTHE iPRESENT iSITUATION	37

OBJECTIVES iOF iBUSINESS iPLAN. — 38

STRATEGIC iPLAN — 39

FINANCIAL iPLAN — 39

STEPS iTO iA iPERFECTLY iWRITTEN iBUSINESS iPLAN — 40

DO RESEARCH.	41
DETERMINE THE REASONS FOR YOUR PLAN.	41
CREATE AN ORGANIZATIONAL PROFILE.	42
DOCUMENT ALL ASPECTS OF YOUR BUSINESS.	42
HAVE A STRATEGIC MARKETING PLAN IN PLACE.	43
YOU NEED TO HAVE A STRATEGIC MARKETING PLAN IN PLACE; THIS WILL HELP IN THE SALES, DISTRIBUTIONS, AND MARKETING PROCESS.	43
MAKE IT ADAPTABLE BASED ON YOUR AUDIENCE.	43
EXPLAIN WHY YOU CARE.	43

CHAPTER 5 — 45

FINANCING YOUR BUSINESS — 45

BUSINESS FINANCING:	45
UNDERSTANDING FINANCING	46

SHORT TERM FINANCING — 46

WHY SHORT TERM FINANCING	46

REASONS FOR SHORT-TERM FINANCE — 47

SOURCES OF SHORT-TERM FINANCE — 47

TRADE CREDIT	48
BANK CREDIT	48
LOANS	48
INSTALLMENT CREDIT	50

LOANS FROM CO-OPERATIVE BANKS — 50

THE DISTINCTION BETWEEN BANK OVERDRAFT AND BANK LOAN 51

DIFFERENCES BETWEEN BANK OVERDRAFT AND CASH CREDIT 51

TYPES OF SECURITIES REQUIRED FOR BANK CREDIT 52

SOURCES OF LONG-TERM FINANCE 55

REASON FOR LONG TERM FUND: 55

FACTORS DETERMINING LONG-TERM FINANCIAL REQUIREMENTS 56

SOURCES OF LONG TERM FUNDING 57

PUBLIC DEPOSITS 66

PROCESS IN RAISING FUNDS THROUGH PUBLIC DEPOSITS. 66
CHARACTERISTICS 67
ADVANTAGES 67

COMMERCIAL BANK LOAN FACILITIES. 69

INTRODUCTION

This book was written with the intent to provide you with a user guide for your new business. We will start with the first step which is by analyzing your business ideas to make sure that it's built on concrete base or ground. We will then look at the legal aspects of securing your thoughts, bringing together your business ideas, and the responsibilities that go with it. We will also look at financing and what investors look for in a business. We will create a financial model analysis and a business plan and finally look at creating the team that will help you meet up with your goals.

Starting your own company is one of the most common dreams that everybody wants in life. The anticipation of being your boss, harvesting the full rewards of your hard work or building something meaningful and controlling your own life, all drive thousands of people to take action each year.

Unfortunately, statistics report that investors invest only in one out of every thousand of the plans they see, the reasons for this failure rate are diverse. However, a considerable deal of responsibility still lies in poor esteem of what is involved in starting a business, poor planning, and a poor understanding of what customers want.

This book will be helpful to anyone who has started or wants to start their own business. It will be particularly useful for a set of people who wish to start an entire business also people who have the ideas but yet to start a business they want to start.

This book has grown from the course but is not intended as a textbook; it is meant to help people who wish to start up a new business, so let's get down to business.

CHAPTER 1

STARTING A BUSINESS

If you're thinking of starting a business, then this is the best book for you to begin with. This is the beginning of an exciting new journey in your life that you'll look back in years from now as the best decision you ever made.
In this book, you will find the information you need to help you to make that happen - information to help and make your new business a successful one.

Therefore, some of the questions I will like to ask you are:

HOW PREPARED ARE YOU TO START A BUSINESS?

Starting a business is different from being an employee. You need a different mindset if your new business is going to be successful.
Part of it is being the big boss and having a whole different set of responsibilities.
While the other part of it is about no longer having the safety net you once had. If you are sick, you can't just call in, and Whatever you were going to do, however, still needs to be done, and there are no medical, insurance, or dental benefits unless you buy them yourself.

AM NOT AN INDUSTRIALIST?

A lot of people that wish to start a new business frequently ask the above-started questions, but "I'd love to start my own business, and I'm not an entrepreneur." I have two things to tell you.

Firstly, what does it mean to be an entrepreneur? However, there is a particular set of features that entrepreneurs commonly share in his or her business.

But secondly, does it even matter if you don't have the "correct" characteristics of an entrepreneur? It's far more essential to be able to answer yes to these questions.

WHY FEAR OF STARTING A BUSINESS?

Why are you putting on fear of starting your own business if it's something you want to do for a living?

People have various answers, but for many, the reasons boil down to fear - fear of the unknown, fear of failure, even fear of success is not uncommon. If this is actually you, however, you should learn how to conquer your fear of starting a business so you can get on with making your dream a reality.

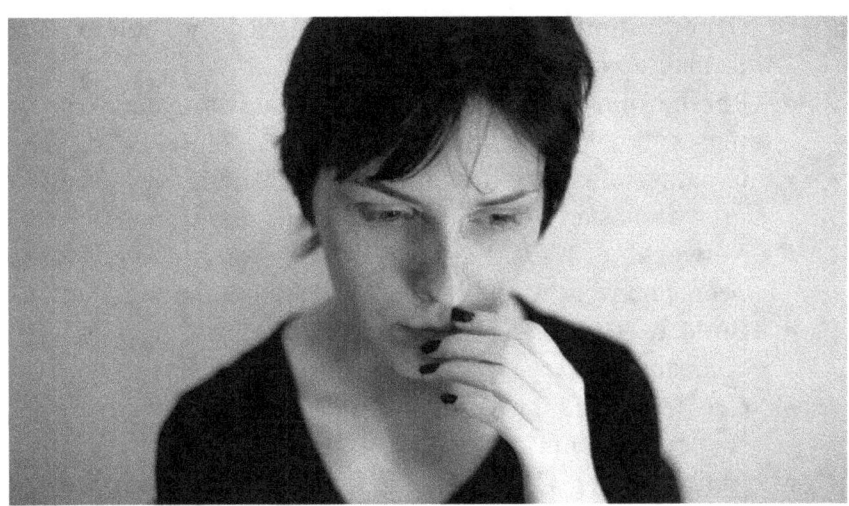

SOME OF THE PURPOSE WHY YOU SHOULD START A BUSINESS.

They are a lot of reasons why many people venture into starting a business. Below are the reasons:

- **Flexibility and Adaptability: It's flexible and** suit your work hours.
- **Free time and Freedom: You have more time to** spend with your relatives, family, and friends. However, this is only applicable once your business is established, and you have employees handling the majority of essential responsibilities. Don't expect to have more time until you reach a certain level. Expect to have *much less.*
- **Rules setting**: policies, therefore making thinks look flexible and straightforward.
- **Deadlines:** No more last-minute rushing except you want to do it.
- **Selling process:** Online? In-person? Inbound? Outbound? It's your call.
- **Organizational culture:** You can set the culture and formalities of your business.
- **Pursue your passion:** You can do whatever that makes you most happy.
- **Create something from scratch:** Watch your business grow from start to finish.
- **Networking:** It creates an opportunity for you to meet new people network with other entrepreneurs and professionals.
- **Build a team:** Decide who to hire and bring into your company.
- **Create jobs:** Improve the economy with job opportunities for people around.
- **Help people:** Use products like goods and services to improve people's lives.
- **Become an expert:** Learn the trend of your industry through firsthand experience.
- **Invest in yourself:** You take the risk of becoming a business owner, and you'll gain the rewards.

- **Make more money:** Your desire to want a pay increment, you can give yourself one or more than.
- **Financial independence:** Only you or one else is signing your paychecks.
- **Tax benefits:** Write off your highest cost while you do get to write off lots of the expenses as an entrepreneur.
- **New challenges every day:** Find a new trend to stimulate your mind peacefully.
- **Get exposed to new cultures:** Discover new opportunities, perspectives, and approaches.
- **Discover new fields:** desire to delve deeper into your industry and discover new opportuinities.
- **Create an asset:** Give you a chance to create an asset.
- **Connect with your clients:** the opportunity to meet new people and clients.
- **Delegate tedious tasks:** Don't do anything you don't want to.
- **You can stop working:** It is possible to stop working and employ someone else
- **The power to give:** Have the strength and flexibility to donate time or money to worthy causes.
- **Get involved in the community:** You can participate actively in social amenities also include activity in your neighborhood and region.
- **Improve your industry:** Desire to push your industry forward with innovations and ideas.
- **Get a mentor:** Meet people of a higher level that are valuable, insightful, and learn from them.
- **Become a mentor:** Take your knowledge and experience, and mentor someone else.
- **Learn new skills:** Desire to learn new skills and acquire new knowledge in your field
- **Attend new classes and seminars:** Attending new courses assist you in Constantly refine your skillset and stay updated.
- **Have a big office:** If you wish the most prominent office in your workplace, it's yours.

- **Work from anywhere:** The desire to work from home, an office, or a beach if you so choose.
- **Have the option for multiple ventures:** Desire to Start another business when you're done with this one.
- **Gain entrepreneurial experience:** Gain knowledge, and also being an entrepreneur makes you a better professional in almost any position.
- **Get recognized:** Recognitions start earning name recognition and build a reputation.
- **Get things done faster:** Set your efficiency rates.
- **Build a personal brand:** Always have the time to develop your brand and tie it into your business.
- **Get more creative:** Create your opportunities and your solutions.
- **Inspire others:** for other people to follow their dreams.
- **Reduce your commute:** It reduces your commute by Find an office space closer to your home.
- **Find pride and fulfillment:** Gaining knowledge above expected. Finally, start taking pride in the work you're doing.
- **Learn to embrace failure:** If you fail, you'll walk away with new skills and more experience you never had before.
- **Leave something behind:** Leaving something behind Pass the business down to your children and grandchildren.
- **Changes:** It may seem like a lofty goal for you right now, but your company really could change the world.
- **Resources:** With the Internet, it's easier than ever to find resources you need, including startup capital, grants, loans, and even mentors.
- **Nothing is stopping you:** What's keeping you from being an entrepreneur? Of course, there are risks, but nothing is forcing you not to take them.

CHAPTER 2

BUSINESS IDEAS

HOW TO FIND BUSINESS IDEAS.

If you're one of those persons who previously have a company idea - great! Leap down to the next section for some input on what type of business to start.

Sometimes the hardest part of commencing a business is coming up with a business idea. Should you pursue your passion? Would it be better to choose a company based on earnings potential? Maybe you need to take in on the subsequent big thing?

Here are some thoughts to spark your creativity and attention so that you can make the best business approach to fit your goals.

SITUATION AND GOAL.

It's essential to consider your circumstance in life when you're scanning through business ideas and perspective; however, the best businesses for the moment might differ if you're beginning a business when you're in bad financial straights.

It's also essentials to put into consideration your goals. Are you looking to start part-time around a job? Some businesses work well for students or also part-timers. Maybe you are on a tight budget and want to make extra earnings moonlighting on the side. Or perhaps you are retired and want a manageable business to help support you during your retirement years.

Perhaps, you want a business or a firm to support your lifestyle goals and also freedom, such as traveling to anywhere in the world. With the Internet, it's easier than ever to become a lifestyle entrepreneur and also have some level of freedom.

INTERESTS AND PASSIONS.

If you are going to establish your career, why not start a business around something you enjoy doing? If you are passionate about protecting the environment, there are many great business ideas, such as eco-friendly product sales and eco-friendly travel services and others.

If you are creative, there are many ways to turn your talents into income, including craft business ideas. Do you love to read? Several business ideas involve books, including book blogging and writing, editing. Or maybe you enjoy animals, in which case there are many opportunities to build a business around pets.

TRENDS AND NEEDS.

Many people start a firm based on the latest business trends, or by filling an untapped need in the marketplace. eBay began to the peer-to-peer marketplace trend that has led to companies such as Airbnb, Etsy, and Uber. You could take this direction to form your peer-to-peer commercial center, maybe in garden hardware rental or shed rentals.

Many initiatives were born out of need, and a few administrations were made to create life simpler. On the off chance that you've ever thought, "It would be decent if someone would make something that...," you might have a business opportunity by making it yourself.

CREATING YOUR BUSINESS IDEAS.

Do you've to have a unique, inventive, never-done-before thought? Whereas that can be hazardous, the bounty of business visionaries has been active with fresh ideas. The individual computer, the iPod, a web bookstore, and the pet shake were all, at one time, unique and innovative ideas. If you need to end up another enhanced business person, you've got to be an alarm to the openings all around you and have the drive to form it works.

NARROWING YOUR OPTIONS.

The most exceptional business thought is the one that's best suited to you, so consider how your identity, interface, and strengths relate to the ideas you're engaging. This can be progressing to be your career, so think whether or not you're willing to stay to it for the long pull until it's successful.

TESTING YOUR BUSINESS IDEAS.

Once you've settled on what you think could be a reasonable trade, check your thoughts maybe when sitting around idly and think about cash to propel the business. Begin with a possibility to think about deciding on the off chance that there's an advertisement for what you need to do. No matter what trade you've chosen, running through a condensed version of commerce arranged is a fabulous way to test your business idea. If for the occasion, your thought was to supply computer administrations and you found that there were as of now eight such businesses in a town with less than 50,000 individuals, you'd know that this trade thought wasn't an incredible choice unless you'll discover a way to stand out from the competition.

SOURCES OF BUSINESS IDEAS

You are wondering how to come up with a business thought? Well, trade thoughts are all around you. A few come from a careful examination of advertising patterns and customer needs; others come from luck. If you're curious about beginning a trade but do not know what item or benefit you might offer, investigating these ways of coming up with a business thought will assist you in selecting.

EXAMINE YOUR OWN SKILL SET FOR BUSINESS IDEAS:

Do you've got ability or demonstrated track record that seems to end up the promise of a profitable business? The other day I talked to a man who had gone through a long time overseeing cleaning administrations at a healing center. Nowadays, he runs his claim active residential and trade cleaning benefit. An ex-logger is presently making his living as a craftsman; he makes "chainsaw figures" out of wood. And the illustrations of experts who have begun their claim organizations or counseling benefit businesses are legion.

To discover reasonable commerce thought, inquire yourself, "What attractive abilities and involvement do I have? Will individuals be willing to pay for my items or services?"

KEEP UP WITH CURRENT EVENT:

If per chance that you observe the news routinely with the cognizant aim of coming up with commerce thought, you will be flabbergasted at how numerous trade openings your brain produces. Keeping up with current occasions will assist you in distinguishing advertise patterns, unused crazes, industry news - and some of the time, honest remaining thoughts that have commerce possibilities. For the event, after same-sex relational unions got to be lawful in Canada, business people started offering visitor travel bundles that incorporate a marriage ceremony to same-sex couples from other countries. Would you have got distinguished that commerce opportunity after you listened that the Canadian marriage laws had changed?

INVENT NEW PRODUCT OR SERVICE:

The key to coming up with business thoughts for an unused item or benefit is to recognize a showcase require that's not being met. For illustration, back in 2004, a Harvard College brain research understudy named Mark Zuckerberg recognized a demand for a campus-wide social-networking site that would permit understudies and staff to share individual profiles and other information.

He went on to create Facebook and got to be one of the most youthful, wealthy people within the world. The blast of versatile gadgets has made a tremendous request for handy apps. In 2008 a combination of young businesspeople named Travis Kalanick and Garrett Camp had inconvenience hailing a cab in Paris. The chosen merely ought to be able to tap a button on your versatile phone and get a ride, and as a result, went on to found Uber. Look around and inquire, "How might this circumstance be made strides?" Inquire individuals almost the new administrations that they'd like to see.

Center on a specific target market and brainstorm thoughts for administrations that gather would be curious about it. For illustration, there are millions of maturing nursery workers over North America. What items or administrations seem you make that would empower them to garden longer and more effectively? Finding a specialty advertise and abusing it is one of the most excellent ways to victory in business.

ADD VALUE TO AN EXISTING PRODUCT:

The distinction between thick wood and wrapped up amble could be a great case of putting an item through an extra handle, which increments its esteem, but additional forms are not the as it were way regard could be included. You might, moreover include administrations, or combine the item with other items. For occasion, a nearby cultivate which offers to create too offers a vegetable conveyance benefit; for an expense, buyers can have a box of new vegetables conveyed to their entryway each week. What commerce thoughts can you create along these lines? Center on what items you might purchase and what you might do to them or with them to do a profitable business.

INVESTIGATE OTHER MARKETS:

Some business thought isn't suited to neighborhood utilization - but offer incredibly to an outside showcase. Sections of the land of wild blueberries encompass my small town. For years the bushes created berries that nourished bears and fowls; B.C. features a flourishing blueberry industry that doesn't take off room for a wild blueberry advertise.

But one business visionary realized that there's a high request for items such as these in Japan - and those same wild blueberries are presently being collected and transported. Finding out around other societies and exploring other showcase openings is a fabulous way to discover commerce thoughts.

IMPROVE EXISTING PRODUCT OR SERVICES:

You know what they say approximately the individual who builds distant a much better mousetrap. That individual might be you! A nearby business visionary has made an moved forward adaptation of the hula band; it's more significant and more substantial, so hula-hoopers can control it more effectively and do more traps. How did she come up with this thought? She thought hula hooping would be a fun thing to do with her girl but found the commercially available item as well flimsy. There are exceptionally few products (or administrations) that can't be moved forward. Begin creating business ideas by looking at the details and administrations you employ and conceptualizing thoughts as to how they can be better.

GET ON THE BANDWAGON:

In some cases, markets surge for no apparent reason; masses of individuals abruptly "need" something, and the coming about request can't be promptly met. For illustration, amid the SARS plague, there was a voracious request for facial mthe worl - and numerous business people capitalized on the demand. A "temporary fad impact" is additionally made by larger social patterns. There's much more of a request for home-care administrations for the elderly than is right now being provided. And the slant for pets to be treated as family individuals proceeds, making a request for all sorts of pet-related administrations that didn't exist decades prior. Look at existing businesses and the items and administrations they offer and decide in case there's a requirement for more of those items or administration, if there is, create commerce thoughts to fit the advertising gap.

TIPS FOR COMING UP WITH BUSINESS IDEAS

Are you brimming with thoughts for beginning a business now? Write your thoughts down. Let them twirl around in your head and condense. And keep an open intellect and proceed to survey everything you examined and listen from an entrepreneurial point of view. You do not need to run with the primary trade thought you think of; you need to find the thought that's best suited to your aptitudes and wants. Dream, think, plan - and you will be prepared to convert that trade thought into the business you've continuously wanted.

HOW TO COME UP WITH A GREAT BUSINESS IDEAS.

You want to start a business, but you don't know where to begin. That's only natural. The process of starting a business can be quite daunting. Here are five great ideas on how to start with a great business idea.

START WITH WHAT YOU LOVE:

A common thread for new entrepreneurs is starting with something they love and believe in, as evidenced in the new businesses at the Women's Entrepreneur Festival.

Tanya Menendez is the co-founder of a company called Maker's Row, which was designed to help American manufacturers source materials and labor from within the States. Though a tough, scrappy market, she says she didn't lose sleep about a competitor thumping her to the punch: "We had assurance in our execution. No one else had lived our lives."

Kara Goldin, chief executive officer and originator of San Francisco base hint Inc., which produces all-natural essence waters, was grateful for the early doubters: "They are like terrible coaches," she said. "They are there to obtain me to show them I can do it."

START WITH SOMETHING PEOPLE NEED:

Can you genuinely begin a business with less than a hundred bucks? Yes, if you center on what individuals require. For case, consider this summer trade idea: There is a bounty of open places that do not have nibble bars, and indeed the comfort store's fair, not helpful sufficient. Bottled water, sports drinks, visors, cheap shades, and battery-powered fans will offer anyplace there's the sun. Attempt parks, the shoreline, baseball home field, or indeed an active road corner close prevalent summer destinations.

START WITH A TWIST:

Rebecca and Daniel Dengrove are the brother-and-sister group that co-founded Brewla, a line of all-natural ice pops that are based on brewed fixings like tea. They have been named "Startup of the Year" by the Divider Road Diary and were included in an arrangement of recordings on that WSJ. "We needed to reengineer a classic, conjointly make it more advantageous," clarified Daniel of the product. As a result, his sister and co-founder could be a nourishment researcher, and their experimentation bore bounty of natural product. And whereas the trade began little (utilizing a cart), the kin presently has their sights set on getting the artisanal ice pop in more retailers across the nation — more on family nourishment businesses here.

START WITH SOMETHING YOU CAN TEST:

The objective of a minimum viable product (MVP) is to test out a trading hypothesis through a rapidly created, stripped-down model of a product that can be brought to showcase quickly and cheaply. Cases incorporate Zappos, which, early on, took photographs of shoes in neighborhood stores, posted them online, and after that bought the shoes from the stores and transported them out rather than building a huge stock. Groupon too propelled with an unimaginably straightforward form of its inevitable everyday bargain mail -- it was mostly a PDF and a WordPress location, to start with.

START WITH SOMETHING YOU CAN DO WITH SIDE.

Jesse Phillips, a co-founder of the calendar company NeuYear, clarifies a "muse" business as such: "a computerized business that gives you your target month to month pay profit, so you'll do what you need." Phillips was exceptionally motivated by Ferriss's book in beginning a company to convey well-designed calendars to assist individuals in tracking and accomplishing their objectives over a year. "We began a new year to help individuals accomplish their dreams," he clarified. "One of the leading ways to center your exertion toward accomplishing your dreams is to arrange and seek after objectives. This doesn't need to be an insane huge or nitty-gritty thing; it's as simple as considering around the steps to realize something, and making due dates for each step." In making a vast, design-focused calendar, he and his cohorts pointed to create that handle as straightforward as possible. Things to consider when choosing what commerce or business you ought to start.

1. **How knowledgeable are you about the business you are considering opening? :**

   What do you know about the products, services, and market? Look at companies that you know very well, and not just from a technical perspective, but from a market standpoint.

2. **Make sure you have all the essential skills to run the business:**

(e.g., not just those required to manufacture the product or deliver the service). Remember, no matter what the business is, you will have to do some selling.

3. **How much money do you have to invest?:**

   Businesses such as graphic design and consulting require far less start-up capital, for instance, than opening a retail establishment. Buying a franchise can be a good idea, but do you have enough capital for both the purchase and the initial running costs?

4. **Imagine about what you take pleasure in doing and what you are zealous about:**

   You are more probable to stay the path and be victorious if you enjoy what you do. Though, be cautious that your obsession for your diversion doesn't blind you to the business potential it has. You may be an exceptional writer of poetry, but building a living from it is all but not viable.

5. **Decide what type of selling might be involved:**

   A retail store, for instance, allows you to be a little like a spider in its web, waiting for people to come along before interacting with them. Being a consultant, on the other hand, means cold calling and attending business mixers. Remember, selling is ALWAYS a significant part of any business.

CHAPTER 3

BUSINESS ENTITY AND TYPES

A business entity is an entity that uses economic resources to provide goods or services to customers in exchange for money or other goods and services.

Business organizations come in different types and various forms of ownership.

Classes of Business

There are three main classes of businesses:

1. Service Business

A service class of business provides intangible commodities *(products with no physical form)*. Service type that offers a different kind of specialized or professional skills, expertise, advice, and other comparable products.

E.g. of service firms are hair salons of a different kind, both male and female, electronic repair shops, schools or collage, a financial institution like banks, accounting firms, and also law firms.

2. Merchandising Business

This class of business purchases products at wholesale value and sells the equivalent or same product at retail price. They are identified as "buy and sell" businesses. They make a gain by selling the goods at rates higher or more than their purchase costs.

A merchandising business sells a product without changing its form. Examples are grocery stores, convenience stores, distributors, and other resellers.

3. Manufacturing Business

Unlike a merchandising business, a manufacturing business buys products to use them as materials in making a new product. Thus, there is a transformation of the products purchased.

A manufacturing business combines *raw materials, labor, and overhead costs* in its production process. The manufactured goods will then be sold to customers.

4. Hybrid Business

Hybrid businesses are companies that may be classified in more than one type of business. A restaurant, for example, combines ingredients in making an excellent feast like a meal (making), sells wine, and fills customer requests.

Classes of Business Organization

These are different classes of business ownership:

1. Sole Proprietorship

A sole proprietorship is defined as a business owned or possessed by only one person or an individual. It is easy or simple to start and is the least expensive in all forms of business. The owner faces *indefinite liability*; meaning, the receivables of the business may go after the personal assets or properties of the owner of the business if he can't pay them.

The sole proprietorship is typically adopted by small business entities that involve just one person's ownership.

2. Partnership

A partnership is a form of a business that is owned by two or more persons or individuals who bring their resources or capital together then invest it into the entity. The partners share the earnings of the business among themselves.

In *partnerships,* partners have limitless liability. In this form of partner called *limited partnerships,* creditors cannot go after the personal assets or properties of the limited partners.

3. Corporation

A corporation is a form of business organization that has a separate legal personality from its owners or is a form of business where the owners are separate from the business entity itself.

The owners (stockholders) benefit from limited liability but have limited participation in the company's operations or running of business activities. The *board of directors,* who are elected by a group of shareholders to oversee the daily activities and also control the operation of the corporation.

However, in addition to those critical forms of business ownership, these are some other classes of organizations that are common in today's world:

4 Limited Liability Company

As the name implied, Limited liability companies (LLCs) are a hybrid class of businesses that have the feature of both a corporation and also a partnership. An LLC is not incorporated; therefore, it is not considered a corporation. But, the owners enjoy a limited level of liability like in a corporation.

Cooperative

A cooperative is an organization owned by a group of individuals or persons and is operated or run for their mutual benefit. The persons or individuals that make up the group are called *members*. Cooperatives may also be incorporated or unincorporated as others.

Some illustrations of cooperatives are water and electricity (utility) cooperatives board, cooperative banking(financial institute), credit unions, and housing cooperatives.

Furthermore:

Association

An Association is a structured group of people usually more than two or more who share in a common interest, purpose, or idea.

Estate

An Estate is usually a Sole Proprietorship and occurs when an individual proprietor passes away. Due to the legality or legitimacy and the operation of the business, it can be put into an estate status so the business can continue or carry on operating under accessible ownership until all legal issues have been determined. An administrator or legal personnel will be assigned or directed to the estate. The business can be estate status for an extended time.

Joint Venture

A Joint Venture is formed for a limited length of time to carry out a business transaction or operation.

Limited Liability Limited Partnership (LLLP)

A Limited Liability Limited Partnership is a Limited Partnership that chooses to become an LLLP by including a statement to that effect in its certificate of a limited partnership. This type of business structure may shield general partners from liability for obligations of the LLLP. Filing with the Washington Secretary of State is required.

Limited Liability Partnership (LLP)

A Limited Liability Partnership (LLP) is similar to a General Partnership except that usually, a partner doesn't have individual liability for the carelessness or even negligence of a different partner. This kind of business structure is used frequently by professionals, such as accountants and lawyers.

Limited Partnership

A Limited Partnership is comprised of one or more general and limited partners. The general partners run the affair of the business and share in its profits and losses while Limited partners share in the profits of the business or company but however, their losses are limited to the level or extent of their invested capital. Limited partners are generally, not participated in the day-to-day running of the business or company.

Massachusetts Trust

A Massachusetts Trust is known as an incorporated business or company of which the properties or assets being held and also managed or controlled by the trustees for the shareholders. The trustees are seen as an employee or staff because they work for the trust.

Municipality

A Municipality is a public corporation build or set-up as a subdivision of a state for a local governmental reason.

Non-profit Corporation

A Non-profit Corporation is also known as a non-profit organization, is a legal firm and is characteristically run to promote an idea or objective rather than in the interests of profit or earning. Many non-profits organizations aim at serving the public interest, but some fit into place in private sector activities. If your non-profit organization is or plans to raise money from the general public, it may also be needed to register with the Charities Program(CP) e. Charitable activities may need additional or extra registration.

Professional Limited Liability Partnership (PLLP)

A PLLP is a limited liability partnership structure designed for licensed professionals. A person or group of persons licensed or otherwise legally authorized to render professional services.

Tenants in Common

A tenant in Common allows two or more people to occupy the same business while retaining separate identities regarding assets or liabilities resulting from business activities.

Trust

A Trust is a legal relationship in which one person, called the trustee, holds property for the benefit of another person, called the beneficiary.

CHAPTER 4

BUSINESS PLANNING

What is a Business Plan?

A Business Plan is a document in which a business prospect or a business already underway is identified, described, and analyzed, examining its technical, economic, and financial feasibility.

The Plan develops all of the measures and strategies necessary to convert the business opportunity into a concrete business project.

It is a necessary tool to start up a business project, independently of the size of the project and of the amount of business experience of the entrepreneur.

A business plan is a written description of your business's future, a document that tells what you plan to do and how you plan to do it. If you jot down a paragraph on the back of an envelope describing your business strategy, you've written a plan or at least the germ of one.

Business plans are innately strategic. You start here, today, with certain resources and abilities and you want to get to there, a point in the future (usually three to five years out), at which period your business will have a different set of resources and abilities as well as greater profitability and increased assets. Your plan shows how you will get from here to there.

Reason for a business plan.

- The reason for a Business Plan is to recognize, describe and analyze a business

- Opportunity and business already in progress, examining its technical, economic, and financial viability.

- Moreover, it should provide as a business card for introducing the business to others: banks, investors, institutions, public bodies or any other agent involved, when it comes
time to seek cooperation or financial support of any kind.

A Business Plan has a dual function:
- Management Tool.
- Planning Tool.
- Management Tool:
- Provides economic/financial projections.
- Enhances the monitoring and control of the business by following up there results obtained and analyzing management indicators.
- Introduces the analysis of supply and demand.
- Reflects the commercial strategy and the marketing policy.
- Identifies the guidelines for the management of human resources.
- Analyzes the key factors of success and the risks of a business.

Planning Tool:
- The company assumes and takes responsibility for the definition of its objectives: With results-oriented actions.
- Strict fulfillment of its economic commitments.
- Orients decision-making processes:
- Provides qualitative and quantitative information.
- Planning conforms to a similar pattern.

why prepare a Business Plan

- Because it provides a global analysis of the business.
- Because it forces us to analyze whether the business project is feasible or not.
- Because it forces us to make a strategic reflection on the business.
- Because it will help to manage the business
- Because it serves as a business card introducing the company.

content of a business plan

The development of a BUSINESS PLAN consists of the following elements, which provide answers to the main questions that can be raised by third parties:

- Analysis of present situation (who are we?)
- Business plan objectives (what do we want to do?).
- Strategic plan(how do we want to do it?)
- Financial plan (how are we going to finance it?)

Analysis of the present situation

- What is the sector like? What are the present situation of the sector and the future outlook?
- Who specifically is the competition in the sector in which the company participates and what?
- Is the degree of contention with competitors? Who are the prospective competitors?
- What are the major factors that decide the achievement or crash of a competitor in the sector?
- In what way is our business diverse from the business of our competitor?
- Recognize weaknesses, threats, strengths, and opportunities of the business.
- Is there a target market for this business?

OBJECTIVES OF BUSINESS PLAN.

- What is the purpose of investing in this business or firm?

- What exactly does my business comprise of? What are the commodities that I am going to offer?

- What strategy am I going to follow to maintain a competitive advantage over?

- Time; specialization, differentiation or competition in costs?

- What areas or processes are critical for the development of the business? What

- Do areas support significant processes of the business or company?

- What are my ideas on the evolution of the business

STRATEGIC PLAN

- Mostly, What is the mission of my business firm?

- What are the tactical lines of my project going to clarify as or over long-term objectives?

- Have precise action plans should be clear for achieving the long-term objectives?

- Have available resources been allocated or directed to such plans to attend its objectives?

- My marketing policy? Have I considered the basic issue of marketing like pricing, place, products, and promotions?

- How many employees do I have has staff? And what are my personnel or top management policies like?

- Have you planned for necessary financial needs that could arise or come up in the long term?

FINANCIAL PLAN

- The purpose is to analyze the profitability and economic feasibility of the business project.

- This analysis is the quantification of the strategy defined by the entrepreneur and will enable him or her to analyze the economic impact of decision making.

- A full analysis includes a projection for the time horizon considered in the business plan.

- Income and Expenditure Projections.

- Investment Budget and Depreciation Schedule.
- Profit and Loss Account.

- Borrowing Requirements.

- Balance Sheet.

- Cash Flow.

- Net Present Value.

Steps to a Perfectly Written Business Plan

Every business needs to have a written business plan. Whether it's to provide direction or attract investors, a business plan is vital for the success of your organization. But how do you write a business plan?

the business plan should include:

- Executive summary -- a picture or snapshot of your business or how your business should look like.
- Company narrative -- describes what you do and more details of the company you presume.
- Market analysis or investigation - research on your sector of kind of business you want to venture into, like the industry, market, and competitors
- Organization and management process -- your business and management structure including all forms of management functions

- Service or product -- the products or services you're offering and what commodities you want
- Marketing and sales –the various ways you wish to market your business to the world to see and your sales strategy
- Financing request -- how much fund you will need for next 2 to 4 years
- Financial projections -- supply information like income statements cash flow and balance sheets
- Appendix – it includes an optional section or parts that includes résumés and permits

though, getting started may be complicated to do. So, here are seven steps for writing a perfect business plan.

Do Research.

"Research and analyze your product, your market, and your objective expertise," William Pirraglia, a now-retired senior financial and management executive, has written. "Consider spending twice as much time researching, evaluating, and thinking as you spend writing the business plan.

"To write the perfect plan, you must know your company, your product, your competition, and the market intimately mostly pricing and promotions."

However, you have to know all you can about your business or company and the industry you are penetrating. Know all you can about your industry or business environment and talk to your audience, supporters, and customers.

Determine the reasons for your plan.

A business plan, as explained by *Entrepreneur,* is a "written document illustrate the nature of the business including the sales and also marketing strategy, and the financial prospects, and containing a projected profit and loss statement." though, your business plan can provide several different purposes.

As it's "also a road map that gives directions so as a business could plan its future and helps it evade bumps in the road." That's essential to retain in mind if you're self-financing or to bootstrap your business or company but, if you want to attract or invite investors, your plan will have a diverse purpose, and you will have to write a plan that cover targets them so it will have to be as clear and succinct as possible. When you identify your plan, make sure you have defined these goals personally as well.

Create an organizational profile.

Creating a profile is important. Your company profile includes the history of your company when it started to date, what commodities you offer, your target market also marketing strategy and spectators, your resources, how you're going to resolve a problem, and what makes your organization exceptional.

Organizational profiles are frequently found on the company's official website and are used to draw potential customers and talent. Though your profile can be used to portray your organization in your business plan, it's not only an essential part of your business plan or idea. However, it's also one of the first written parts of the plan.

Having your business outline or profile in place makes this pace a whole lot easier to create.

Document all aspects of your business.

Investors desire to make sure that your business or company is going to make the earnings. Because of this anticipation, investors desire to know the whole thing about your business. To assist with this procedure, document everything from your expenses or costs, cash flow(cash in and out), and industry projections. As well as, don't forget minor details like your location strategy and licensing agreements.

Have a strategic marketing plan in place.

You need to have a strategic marketing plan in place; this will help in the sales, distributions, and marketing process.

Make it adaptable based on your audience.

"The prospective readers of a business plan are a different bunch, ranging from professional bankers and venture capitalists to staff," states *Entrepreneur.* "even though this is a diverse group, it is a limited one. And each class of reader does have certain usual interests. If you recognize these interests in advance, you can be certain to consider them when actually preparing a plan for that certain audience."

For illustration, bankers will be more interested in financial position and cash-flow statements, while venture capitalists will be looking at the essential business concept or ideas and your management team. The manager who is part of your team will be using the plan to "remind themselves of objectives or goals."

However, because of this reason, ensure that your plan can be modified depending on the audience who is reading your plan. However, keep these alterations restricted from one plan to another. in this way, when sharing monetary projections, you should keep that data the same across the board.

Explain why you care.

Whether or not you are sharing your plan with an investor or someone who is interested in investing, customer or team member even client, your plan requires to prove that you're passionate or zealous and dedicated, and you truly care about your business and the business plan. You could converse the mistakes that you have learned, list the problems that you're hoping to resolve, describe your economic values, and set up what makes you stand out from the competition. When I initially started my payments company, I set out to overcome the world. I needed to change the way payments were made and make it easier for anyone, anywhere in the world to pay anyone with few to no fees. I explained why I wanted to build this. My passion shows through everything I do.

By explaining why you care about your business, you create an emotional connection with others so that they'll support your organization going forward.

CHAPTER 5

FINANCING YOUR BUSINESS

Business Financing:

Financing is required to set up a business and raise it to profitability. There are numerous sources to think of when looking for a start-up fund. But first, you require to consider how much money you need and when you will need it. The financial needs of a company will vary according to the category and size of the business. For instance, processing businesses are generally capital intensive, requiring huge amounts of capital. Retail businesses usually need less capital. Debt and equity are the two main sources of financing. Government grants to finance certain aspects of a business may be an alternative. Also, incentives may be available to find in certain communities and support activities in particular industries.

Financing is the method of providing finance for business activities, making purchases, or investing. Financial institutions such as banks are in the business of providing capital to the company, consumers, and investors to help them attain their goals. The use of financing is very important in any economic structure, as it allows businesses to purchase products out of their urgent reach. Financing is key to the Fund era's business model, for instance. It is difficult to gain financing while in financial distress.

Put differently; financing is a way to leverage the Time value of money (TVM) to put future estimated money flows to use for projects started today. Financing also takes advantage of the fact that some will have an excess of money that they wish to put to work to generate income, while others require money to embark on investment (also with the hope of generating returns), creating a market for the money.

Understanding Financing

There are two main classes of financing available for companies: equity and debt. Debt is a loan that must be paid back often with interest. It usually comes with a certain period, mostly short or long term debt, but it is usually cheaper than raising capital because of tax deduction considerations. Equity does not require to be paid back, but it relinquishes ownership stakes to the shareholder. Both debt and equity have their merits and demerits. Most businesses use a combination of both to finance operations.

SHORT TERM FINANCING

The desire for finance may be for long-term, medium-term, or for short-term. Financial necessities about fixed and working capital vary from one organization to another. To meet out these necessities, funds require to be raised from various sources. Some sources, like the issue of shares and debentures, offer funds for a longer time. These are hence, known as sources of long-term finance. However, sources like trade credit, cash credit also overdraft, and bank loan facilities, etc. which allow money available for a shorter range of time are called sources of short-term finance.

Why short term financing

After the set-up of business, funds are required to meet its day to day expenses. For instance, raw materials must be purchased at expected intervals; workers must be paid wages regularly, water and power charges have to be paid regularly. Thus there is a continuous process necessity of liquid cash to be available for meeting these expenses. For financing such necessities, short-term funds are required. The availability of short-term funds is important. Lack of short-term funds may even lead to the shutting down of a business.

Reasons for Short-term finance

1. It fastens the smooth running of business operations by meeting day to day financial needs.

2. It makes firms to hold stock of raw materials and finished products.

3. With the accessibility of short-term finance, goods can be sold on credit. Sales are for a certain period, and the collection of money from debtors takes time. During this time gap, production continues, and money will be required to finance various day to day of the business.

4. Short-term finance usually becomes more important when it is essential to increase the volume of production during a short period.

5. Short-term funds are also necessary to allow the flow of funds during the operating cycle. The operating cycle refers to the time gap between the beginning of production and realization of sales.

Sources of Short-term Finance

There are several sources of short-term finance which are listed below:

1. Trade credit

2. Bank credit – Loans and advances – Cash credit – Overdraft – Discounting of bills.

3. Customers' advances.

4. Installment credit.

5. Loans from co-operatives.

Trade credit

Trade credit could be defined as a credit granted to manufacturers and traders by the suppliers of raw material, finished goods, components, etc. typically, business enterprises buy supplies on a 30 to 90 days credit. This means that the goods are delivered, but payments are not made until the end of the period of credit. This type of credit does not make the funds available in cash, but it facilitates purchases without making instant payment. This is reasonably the most popular source of finance.

Bank credit

banks grant short-term finance to business firms, which are recognized as bank credit. When bank credit is granted, the borrower gets a right to draw the amount of credit at one time or in installments as and when required. Bank credit may be granted by way of loans, cash credit, overdraft, and discounted bills.

Loans

When a certain amount is advanced by a bank repayable after a specified period, it is known as a bank loan. Such advance is credited to a separate loan account, and the borrower has to pay interest on the whole amount of loan irrespective of the amount of loan actually drawn. Usually, loans are granted against the security of assets.

(i) Cash Credit

It is an agreement whereby banks allow the borrower to withdraw money up to a specified limit. This limit is known as a cash credit limit. At first, this limit is granted for one year. This limit can be extended after review for another year. Though, if the borrower still wants to proceed with the limit, it must be changed after three years. The rate of interest is different depending upon the amount of impulse on the limit.

Banks ask for collateral or assets as security for the grant of cash credit. In this agreement, the borrower can withdraw, payback, and again withdraw the amount within the sanctioned limit impulse. Interest is paid or charged only on the amount withdrawn and not on the amount of entire limit

(iii) Overdraft

An overdraft occurs when a bank allows its depositors or account holders to withdraw money in surplus of the balance in his account up to a precise limit, it is called an overdraft facility. This limit is settled purely based on the credit-worthiness of the borrower. Banks usually give the limit up to Rs.20,000. In this system, the borrower has to show a positive balance in his account on the last Friday of every month. Interest is charged only on the overdrawn money. The rate of interest in the case of overdraft is less than the rate charged under cash credit.

(ii) Discounting of Bill

Banks also offer advance money by discounting bills of exchange, promissory notes, and bundles. When these documents are accessible before the bank for discounting, banks credit the amount to the customer's account after deducting discount. The amount of discount is the same as the amount of interest for the period of the bill.

Installment credit

Installment credit is one of the if not the most acceptable and popular source of finance for consumer goods like television, refrigerators also for industrial goods. You might be aware or inform of this system. Only a small amount of funds is paid at the time of delivery of such articles. The remaining balance of money is paid in a certain number of installments. The dealer charges interest in extending credit. The amount of interest is included while deciding on the amount of installment also another related system is the hire purchase system under which the buyer becomes the owner of the goods after a certain period and full payment of the last installment. Sometimes commercial banks also grant installment credit if they have suitable arrangements with the suppliers.

Loans from Co-operative Banks

They are a good source to acquire short-term finance. Such banks have been established at local, district, and state levels. District Cooperative Banks is the federation of primary credit societies. The State Cooperative Bank finances and controls the District Cooperative Banks in the state. They are also controlled by the Reserve Bank of India regulations. Some of these banks, like the Vanish Co-operative Bank, was initially established as a co-operative society and later renewed into a bank. These banks grant loans for personal as well as business purposes. Membership is the primary condition for securing the loan. The functions of these banks are largely comparable to the functions of commercial banks.

The distinction between Bank Overdraft and Bank Loan

a) Interest Charges: Interest is charged only on the overdrawn amount in the case of bank overdraft, but in the case of bank loan, interest is charged on the entire amount of loan.

b) Amount of lending: The amount of borrowing is restricted in case of bank overdraft, except bank loan could be for any amount depending on the method of which the securities offered by the borrower against the loan.

c) To renew the procedure: The renewal of the procedure is very straightforward in the case of an overdraft. Banks entail positive stability to be shown in the customer's account on the last Friday of every month, but however, loans are to be paid back after the end of the credit period. For renewal, fresh dialogue are to be made.

d) Security: Overdraft instrument is usually offered by banks solely based on credit merit of the customer, but for bank loan security of tangible assets is an important obligation besides the personal security of the borrower.

e) Rate of interest: Rate of interest is usually more than in case of a bank loan.

f) Simplicity and Flexibility: Bank overdraft is more easy to collect than a bank loan. The fund can also be withdrawn deposited and again withdrawn within the confines, but however, in case of a bank loan, the amount approved is fixed.

Differences between Bank Overdraft and Cash Credit

a) Cash credit is a separate agreement of credit granted by a bank to a firm. The firm may or may not have an account with the bank. Overdraft is granted to an account holder purely based on his credit-worthiness. The credit value is decided by the financial reliability of past dealings of the customer with the bank.

b) In case of cash credit, the amount of credit is placed in a separate account of the borrower. Overdraft limit is generally granted to an existing account of the customer.

c) The amount of credit in case of cash credit depends upon the value of securities offered. But overdraft limit is decided on the average balance of the customer in his account. d) Overdraft is granted without the security of tangible assets.

Types of Securities required for Bank credit

Loans and advances are granted by the bank on the personal security of the borrower as well as on the security of some tangible assets besides the standing of the firm. Thus securities against bank credit may be of two types:

(i) Personal security
(ii) Security of tangible assets.

Personal security means the credit-worthiness of the borrower. The worthiness of the borrower based on his financial soundness and past dealings with the bank.

Banks accept the following tangible assets for extending short term finance:

a) Moveable goods :

    Banks accept stock of raw materials and finished goods as security against bank credit. In the case of nonpayment, these goods are sold, and banks recover money.

b) Shares and stock :

Shares and stock that are quoted on a recognized stock exchange are accepted as security against bank credit. The borrower is required to deposit the share certificate along with a transfer deed signed by him.

c) Documents of title to goods :

Bill of lading, Railway Receipts (RR), Goods Receipt (GR), Warehouse warrant are various documents that are recognized as documents of title to goods. To protect credit from the bank, the customer may keep any of these credentials with the bank after suitably endorsing the equal in favor of the bank. This allows the bank to take the goods in case of non-compliance in repayment.

d) Fixed deposit receipts :

It is a form of receipt generally issued by financial institute such as banks as proof of fixed deposits made by the client. Banks give loans to people as a result of the security of this receipt. The interest charged on loan is higher than the interest allowed on deposit. Banks sometimes grant a loan up to 70% of the value of such receipts that appeared on the fixed deposit.

e) Life insurance policies :

Financial institute such as Banks sometimes extends credit based on life insurance policy obtain up to the amount of surrender value of such receipts.

f) Jewelry or precious metals :

This form of security may offer to loan money for private for business purposes. Proprietary concerns sometimes offer jewelry or other valuable metals to get credit.

g) Other securities :

Besides the assets and documents mentioned above, banks also accept National Savings Certificate (NSC), Indira Vikas Patra (IVP), Kisan Vikas Patra (KVP) to grant short-term credit.

What you should Know:

Short-term finance is needed by business firms to meet day to day expenses. It facilitates the smooth running of business operations. It enables the holding of stocks of raw materials and finished products, helps to increase the volume of production at short notice, and bridges the time gap between commencement of production and realization of sales. Sources of Short-term Finance.

Short-term finance is helpful to business in meeting temporary requirements of funds without a heavy burden of interest. It is a flexible source of finance. When necessary, it may also serve long-term purposes through renewal. However, interest has to be paid on short-term borrowing, irrespective of profit, or loss.

It also needs the security of assets to be provided by the borrower. Trade credit is available only in connection with the purchase of raw materials and finished goods. Bank credit can be used for any purpose. No security is required to be provided to avail of trade credit.

Bank credit is usually granted against the security of assets. Bill discounting, as a source of finance has certain advantages and disadvantages. Cash is immediately available without the necessity of any security. No payment is involved unless the bill is dishonored by the drawer. However, interest is due in advance using a discount.

The facility is accessible on the method of the customer's credit merit. Bank overdraft varies from bank loan with reverence to interest payable, amount of credit accessible, security needed, renewal procedure, and flexibility of use. However, differences between bank overdraft and cash credit lie based on two arrangements.

Overdraft is offered to an account holder based on his credit merit and average account balance. The cash credit limit is determined depending on the amount of security offered. Bank credit is granted offered in either the personal security of the borrower or clients or the security of tangible assets or both. Tangible securities may comprise of movable goods also shares and stock, documents of title to goods, fixed deposit receipt, life insurance policy, jewelry, or savings certificates.

SOURCES OF LONG-TERM FINANCE

Long Term Finance – It's meaning and purpose

A company needs funds to purchase a fixed property like land and building, plant and machinery, furniture, etc. These assets may be regarded as the establishment of a business. The capital required for these assets is known as **fixed capital**. A part of the working capital is also of a stable nature.
Funds needed for this part of the working capital and fixed capital are called long term finance.

Reason for long term fund:

The long term finance is required for the following reason:

1. **To Finance fixed assets :**

The company needs fixed assets like machines, buildings, furniture, etc. Finance needed to buy these assets is for a long period, because such assets can be used for a long period and are not for resale.

2. **To finance the permanent part of working capital:**

Business is a continuing activity. It must have a certain amount of working capital, which would be required again and again. This part of working capital is of a fixed or permanent nature. This requirement is also met from long term funds.

3. To fund growth and expansion of business:

The expansion of business needs an investment of a huge amount of capital permanently or for a long period.

Factors determining long-term financial requirements

The amount required to meet the long term capital needs of a company depend upon a lot of factors.

These are :

(a) Nature of Business:

The nature and character of a business determine the amount of fixed capital. A manufacturing company requires land, building, machines, etc. So it has to invest a big amount of capital for a long period But a trading concern dealing in, say, washing machines will need a smaller amount of long term funds because it does not have to purchase buildings or machines.

(b) Nature of goods produced:

If a business is engaged in manufacturing, small and simple clothing will require a smaller amount of fixed capital as compared to one heavy manufacturing machines or heavy consumer items like cars, refrigerators, etc. which will need more fixed capital.

(c) Technology used:

In a big industry like steel, the fixed capital investment is bigger than in the case of a business producing plastic jars using simple technology or producing goods using the labor-intensive technique.

Sources of long term funding

The main sources of long term finance are as follows:

1. Shares:

These are issued to the general public. These may be of two types:(i) Equity and (ii) Preference. The holders of shares are the owners of the business.

2. Debentures:

These are also issued to the general public. The holders of debentures are the creditors of the company.

3. Public Deposits :

The general public also like to deposit their savings with a popular and well-established company which can pay interest periodically and pay-back the deposit when due.

4. Retained earnings:

The company may not give out the whole of its earnings among its shareholders. It may retain a part of the earnings and utilize it as capital.

4. Term loans from banks:

A lot of industrial development banks, cooperative banks, and Commercial banks grant medium-term loans for a period of three to five years.

5. A loan from financial institutions:

There are numerous specialized financial institutions established by the Central and State governments which give long term loans at a rational rate of interest. Some of these institutions are:
Industrial Finance Corporation of India (IFCI), Industrial Development Bank of India (IDBI), Industrial Credit and Investment Corporation of India (ICICI), Unit Trust of India (UTI), State Finance Corporations, etc.

Shares

The issue of shares is the main source of long term finance. Shares are issued by joint-stock companies to the public. A company divides its capital into units of definite face value, say of Rs. 10

each or Rs. 100each. Each unit is called a share. A person holding shares is called as shareholders.

Features of shares:

The main characteristics of shares are the following:

1. It is a unit of the capital of the company.

2. Each share is of specific face value.

3. A share certificate is issued to a shareholder signifying the number of shares and the sum.

4. Each share has a different number.

5. The face value of a share indicates the interest of a person in the company, and the extent of his liability.

6. Shares are transferable units. Investors are of different habits and temperament. Some want to take a smaller risk and are concerned with a regular income. Others may take greater risk in anticipation of huge profits in the future. To tap the savings of different types of people, a company may issue different types of shares. These are:
1. Preference shares, and

2. Equity Shares.

Preference Shares :

Preference Shares are the shares that bring preferential rights over the equity shares. These rights are

(a)   Receiving dividends at a fixed rate,

(b) Getting back the capital in case the company is wound-up. Investments in these shares are safe, and a preference shareholder also gets the dividend
Regularly.

Equity Shares:

Equity shares are shares that do not benefit from any preferential right in the matter of payment of dividends or repayment of capital.

The equity shareholder gets dividends only after the payment of dividends to the preference shares. There is no fixed rate of dividend for equity shareholders. The rate of dividend depends upon the surplus profits. In case of winding up of a company, the equity share capital is refunded only after refunding the preference share capital. Equity shareholders have the right to take part in the management of the company. However,
equity shares also carry more risk.

Following are the merits and demerits of equity shares:

(a) Advantages
(A) To the shareholders:

1. In case there are good earnings, the company pays a dividend to the equity shareholders at a higher rate.

2. The value of equity shares goes up in the stock market with an increase in profits of the concern.

3. Equity shares can be easily sold in the stock market.

4. Equity shareholders have better say in the management of a company as they are conferred voting rights by the Articles of Association.

(B) To the Management:

1. A company can raise fixed capital by issuing equity shares without creating any charge on its fixed assets.

2. The capital raised by issuing equity shares is not required to be paid back during the lifetime of the company. It will be paid back only if the company is wound up.

3. There is no liability on the company regarding payment of dividend on equity shares. The company may announce dividends only if there are enough earnings.

4. If a company raises more capital by issuing equity shares, it leads to greater confidence among the investors and creditors.

Disadvantages:

A) To the shareholders

1. Doubtfulness about payment of dividend:

Equity share-holders get dividend only when the business is earning enough profits, and the Board of Directors declare a dividend.

If there are preference shareholders, equity shareholders get dividends only after payment of dividends to the preference shareholders.

2. Speculative:

Often there is speculation on the prices of equity shares. This is particularly so in times of boom when dividend paid by the companies is high.

1. **Risk of overcapitalization:**

the management miscalculates the long term financial requirements, and it may raise more funds than required by issuing shares. This may amount to over-capitalization
which, in turn, leads to a low value of shares in the stock market.

2. **Possession in name only:**

The holding of equity shares in a company makes the holder one of the owners of the company. Such shareholders enjoy voting rights. They manage and control the company but then it is all in theory. In practice, a handful of persons control the votes and manage the company. Moreover, the decision to declare dividends rests with the Board of Directors.

3. **Higher Risk :**

Equity shareholders bear a very high degree of risk. In case of losses, they do not get a dividend. In case of winding up of a company, they are the very last to get a refund of the money invested. Equity shares actually swim and sink with the company.

B) To the Management

1. No trading on Shares:

Buying and selling on shares mean the ability of a company or firm to increase funds through preference shares, debentures, and bank loan facilities, etc.
On that type of funding, the company has to pay at a fixed rate means the rate remains unchanged. This allows shareholders to enjoy a higher rate of earnings when the gain is large for that period. The main part of the profit earned is paid to the shareholders because borrowed funds carry only a fixed rate of interest, but if a company has only equity shares and does not have

either preference shares, debentures or loans, it cant have the merits of trading(buying and selling) on shares.

2. Conflict of interest:

As the equity shareholders bear voting rights, groups are formed to corner the votes and grab the control of the company. There develops a conflict of interests that is
destructive for the smooth performance of a company.

Debentures

Whenever a firm wants to borrow a huge amount of money for a long period, but a fixed period, it can borrow from the general public by issuing loan certificates called Debentures. The total amount to be borrowed is separated into units of fixed amount say of Rs.100 each. These units are known as Debentures. These are accessible to the public to subscribe to the same method as is done in the case of shares. A debenture is issued under the common seal of the company. It is a written acknowledgment of money that specifies the terms and conditions, such as rate of interest, timely repayment, security offered, etc.

Features of Debenture

Following are the characteristics of Debentures:

i) Debenture holders are the creditors of the company. They are entitled to a periodic sum of interest at a fixed rate.

ii) Debentures are repayable after a fixed period, say five years or seven years as per agreed terms.

iii) Debenture holders do not carry voting rights.

iv) usually, debentures are secured. In case the company fails to pay interest on debentures or repay the initial capital amount, the debenture holders can recover it from the sale of the assets of the business.

Classes of Debentures:

Debentures may be classified as:
a) Redeemable Debentures and Irredeemable Debentures
b) Convertible Debentures and Non-convertible Debentures.

Redeemable Debentures:

These are debentures repayable on a pre-determined date or at any time previous to their maturity, provided the company so desires and gives notice to that outcome.

Irredeemable Debentures:

This is also called perpetual debentures. A company is not bound to repay the amount during its lifetime. If the issuing business fails to pay the interest, it has to redeem such debentures.

Convertible Debentures:

The holders of these debentures are given the alternative to convert their debentures into equity shares at a time and in a ratio as decided by the company.

Non-convertible Debentures:

These debentures cannot be converted into shares.

Merits of debentures:

Following are some of the advantages of debentures:

1) Raising finances without allowing control over the company:
Debenture holders have no right either to vote or take part in the running of the company.

2) A trustworthy source of long term finance:
Since debentures are usually issued for a fixed period, the Company can make the best use of the money. It helps long term
Planning.

3) Tax Benefits:
Interest paid on debentures is treated as an expense and is charged to the profits of the business. The company thus saves income tax.

4) Investors' Safety:
Debentures are mostly protected. On winding up of the company, they are repayable before any payment is made to the shareholders. Interest on debentures is payable irrespective of gain or loss.

Disadvantages:

Following are the demerits of debentures:

1. As the interests of debentures have to be paid every year, whether there are profits or not, it becomes burdensome in case the company incurs losses.

2. Frequently the debentures are safe. The company creates a charge on its assets in support of debenture holders. So a

company that does not own enough fixed assets cannot borrow money by issuing debentures. Moreover, the property of the company, once mortgaged, cannot be used for further lending.

3. Debenture-finance enables a company to trade on equity. But too much of such finance leaves little for shareholders, as most of the earnings may be necessary to pay interest on debentures. This brings dissatisfaction in the minds of shareholders, and the value of shares may fall in the securities markets.

4. Burdensome in times of gloominess. During the depression the profits of the company decrease. It may be difficult to pay interest on debentures. As interest goes on accumulating, it may cause the closure of the company. Until now, you have learned about the issue of shares and debentures as two main sources of raising long term finance. You have also learned about the merits and demerits of the two.

Public Deposits

When modern banks were not there, people used to deposit their savings with business concerns of good character. Even today, it is a very popular and convenient way of raising medium-term finance. The period for which business undertakings accept public deposits ranges between six months to three years.

Process in raising funds through public deposits.

An undertaking that wants to raise funds through public deposits needs to advertise in the newspapers. The advertisement highlights the achievements and upcoming prospects of the undertaking and invites the investors to deposit their savings with it.

It declares the rate of interest, which may differ depending upon the period for which money is deposited. It also declares the time and method of payment of interest and their payment of deposits. A depositor may get his cash back before the date of refund of deposits or which he will have to give notice in advance.

Characteristics:

1. Those deposits are not protected.

2. They are accessible for a period ranging involving six months and 3years.

3. They carry a fixed rate of interest.

4. They do not require complex legal official procedures as are necessary in the case of shares or debentures.

4. Keeping in view the malpractices of certain companies, such as not paying interest for years jointly and not refunding the money, the Government has framed certain rules and regulations regarding inviting the public to deposit their savings and accepting them.

Advantages

Following are the merit of public deposits:

1. straightforward and easy:

The practice of borrowing money through public deposit is very simple and straightforward; It does not need any legal official procedure. It has to be

Advertised in the newspapers and a receipt is to be issued.

2. No charge on assets :

Public deposits are not secured. They do not have any charge on the fixed assets of the company.

3. Inexpensive and Cheap :

Expenses incurred on loan through public deposits are much less than expenses of other sources like shares and debentures.

4. Flexibility :

Public deposits bring flexibility in the formation of the capital of the company. These can be increased when required and refunded when not necessary.

Disadvantages

Following are the demerits of public deposits:

1. Ambiguity:

anxiety should be of high character and have a high credit rating to attract the public to deposit their savings. There may be rapid Withdrawals of deposits which may create financial problems.

2. Uncertainty:

Public deposits do not have any charge on the assets of the concern. It may not always be safe to deposit savings with companies, particularly those who are not very sound.

2. Lack of desirability for professional investors :

As the rate of return is low, and there is no capital appreciation, the specialized investors do not value this mode of Investment.

4. Too costly:

The rate of interest paid on public deposits may be low but then there are other operating costs like commission and brokerage which
make it too costly.

5. Difficulty in the growth of capital-market :

If more and more money is deposited with the companies in this type, there will be less investment in securities. Hence the capital market will not grow. This will deny both the companies and the investors of the benefits of good securities.

6. Over–capitalization :

As it is a straightforward, convenient, and cheaper source of raising money,
companies may have more money than is necessary. In that case, it may not be able to make the best use of the money or may indulge in speculative behavior.

Commercial Bank Loan facilities.

Usually, not all banks, mostly commercial banks in India that award long term borrowing. They grant loans only for a short period, not above one year, but in recent times they have started giving loans for a long period. Commercial banks give term loans, i.e., for more than one year. The period of repayment of the short term loan is extended at intervals, and in some cases, borrowing is given directly for a long period. Commercial banks provide long term finance to small scale units in the priority sector.

Long-term loan from Commercial Banks.

Advantages:

The merits of long-term borrowing from banks are as follows.

1. It is an elastic or flexible source of funding as the borrowing can be payback when the need is met.

2. Finance is obtainable for a definite era or time; hence it is not an unending burden.

3. Banks keep the financial operations of their clients secret.

4. Less time and cost are involved as compared to the issue of Shares and Debentures.

5. Banks do not obstruct the internal affairs of the borrowing Concern, hence the management retains also be in charge of the company.

6. Loans can be paid-back in easy, mostly installments.

7. In the case of small-scale industries and industries in villages and backward areas, the interest charged is low.

Disadvantages:

Followings are the demerits of borrowing from commercial banks:
1. Banks always need personal guarantee or undertaking of assets as collateral and whereas the company cannot increase further loans on these assets.

2. In case the short term borrowings are unmitigated; furthermore, there is always an ambiguity about his continuity process.

3. Too many rules and regulations or documentations are to be satisfied in receiving loans from banks. These formalities make the borrowings from banks, at times, unbearable and difficult.

www.ingramcontent.com/pod-product-compliance
Lightning Source LLC
Chambersburg PA
CBHW060437220526
45465CB00008B/3174